WASHINGTON HEIGHTS

WASHINGTON HEIGHTS
IN SEARCH OF THE VEIL

Jimmy Stalikas

Washington Heights

Copyright © 2022 by James Stalikas. All rights reserved.

No part of this publication may be reproduced, stored in a retrieval system or transmitted in any way by any means, electronic, mechanical, photocopy, recording or otherwise without the prior permission of the author except as provided by USA copyright law.

The opinions expressed by the author are not necessarily those of URLink Print and Media.

1603 Capitol Ave., Suite 310 Cheyenne, Wyoming USA 82001
1-888-980-6523 | admin@urlinkpublishing.com

URLink Print and Media is committed to excellence in the publishing industry.

Book design copyright © 2022 by URLink Print and Media. All rights reserved.

Published in the United States of America
ISBN 978-1-68486-240-5 (Paperback)
ISBN 978-1-68486-239-9 (Digital)

01.07.22

I could see myself from a ceiling elevation being born to a lady with dark hair. I could describe the scissors and the hands that cut my umbilical cord. The next thing I remember I'm sitting on the floor eating a stick of butter that was more like a blur. I was about six years old. I remember going up to the roof when we lived on 172st Amsterdam, and it was snowing. I was up early, so I went up to the roof. Wow! There was so much snow. Once I got off the roof landing and went to the roof's edge, I started to roll a little snowball that grew to the size of a basketball and looked over, and it was clear as soon as I let the snowball fall off the ledge of the roof a lady came into view. God, I just miss her. It was the size of a basketball. Thank god I didn't hit her. Then she looked up, and I know she saw me, Wow! That was a close one.

That's how my life went—feeling scared yet excited. That's how it went—a feeling of excitement of getting away with stuff, and I like it.

So I ran back to the apartment and laid in bed. I was scared shit that someone would be knocking on the door; my father would kick my ass. Around that time my mother and father were on the outs; it was only a matter of time before my dad would be leaving. Mother got tired of his drinking and spending all the money after so many years working at the Plaza Hotel before he went into the service. It was in the navy when the war broke out. He was a torpedo man. After the service, he became a bus driver, I always thought that it was cool being a torpedo man. I would wear his shirt that had a torpedo on it. That meant he sunk a ship. He became a bus driver in the city for MTA.

I remember as a kid my brother and I would go with my father; he would have the Amsterdam line, and my brother and I would go on his bus ride until my mother seen that he was drinking and driving. She put a stop to that, not to mention the passengers my brother and I were riding with our dad was something of the pass. Even as of today, I see the wall that my father ran into when he was drinking and driving down the FDR Highway local streets 116st. That's where my mother yelled at him and took my brother and I out of the car because my father was drinking and driving. Every time I pass that wall, I remember that. Today I passed that wall; that's my route going home from the BX. Living in the city, I could only imagine how my mother felt and what she went through with my dad. To top it off, the misery I must have put her through is another story. My father's drinking became a real problem for my mom. She decided that she can't depend on my dad for an income, so she applied for a job in Columbia Presbyterian Hospital on 168th Broadway Street. One day, I'm playing in the street and saw my Mom coming down the street. She seemed to be so happy, and she was wearing her uniform. Mister Softee music was playing. I ran to my mom and asked if she could buy me ice cream, and she did. That was one of the happiest days I can remember growing up.

    I was coming up on my eighth birthday. Mother brought me a Yogi Berra bat number 8 for my birthday on April 2. My sister Angela's birthday is April first—April Fool's Day—and we would joke around saying she's born a fool and would laugh it off.

    My mom would have a party for my sister. She would always say, "It's Jimmy's birthday tomorrow." She would always celebrate our birthdays together, so I always felt I got beat out of a birthday. I didn't really give a sh——t; no big deal! Besides my sister's girl friends would come, and I like that. They were sweet. I became more interested in things that the grown-ups didn't like, like people stealing or shoplifting.

    I remember it was my eighth birthday, and my sister Rose said, "Come, Jimmy. Be like a bull. Olé!" So I ran towards the towel she had out and when I got there, she moved, and I ran right into the stereo.

My head started to bleed, so my mom took me to the hospital. I got eight stitches on my eighth birthday. How f——g great that is! So I spent the better time of my eigth birthday in the hospital where I was born. I felt really bad, but my mother always tried to make the best of it by buying me a Milky Way.It wasn't that bad; I had cake at home. I'm good and being that it was my birthday, I would let everyone think that I felt bad. But deep down inside, I really didn't give a sh——t; sh——t happens.

This was kind of the way my life went, and I was only eight. That's the time I got left back in the third grade; I was going to PS 173 on Ft. Washington Avenue. My teacher—I would never forget that b——c. I remember I was in a play and no one from my family came; I forgot my lines but made some up. After the play, we got a standing ovation, and everyone said how good I did. I felt good about the play, but deep down inside, I was feeling really bad that my brother or sisters didn't show up. Mom and Dad were working. My dad—well, I didn't know where he was. And around that time, President Kennedy was assassinated, and everyone in class was crying.I was kind of glad we got out of school early and was making fun of the crybabies because at the time, I wasn't comfortable in my skin and couldn't put my finger on it. But every time I drank or did drugs,I felt a lot better, and the feeling stayed with me for years and years to come, having now balance in my life. Going from crisis to crisis was a way of life.

My sister Angela, my sweet sister may her soul rest in peace. As a kid, my brother and I would call her the warden because she use to make my brother and I clean the house, and she'll sit on her fat a——s drinking soda and eating potato chips while getting all the credit from my mom when she got home. So one day, I told her to go eff herself, and she pulled my hair, smacked me around, made me cry. I said eff, this got my bat number eight, and went after my sister saying, "I'm gonna kill you. I'm gonna get you." She ran into the bathroom, locked the door, and said, "No, Jimmy." I kept saying while banging on the door, "I'm gonna kill you." As I was crying, my tears turned into laughter all the way right out the house.When I got home that evening, nothing was said. My mom said that I did a good job. Angela looked at me scared, and I just brushed it off. We are cool now. I didn't tell her that, but she knows better now. That was the last time I had to clean the house. I remember there was ten dollars on the table, and I took it with me to school. I was acting like a show-off counting it in school. Wouldn't you believe my sister Rosie's boyfriend was a junkie. He would come to Mother's house selling all kinds of things.I remember he brought some duffle coats, and my mother brought me a gray one that was a good coat. I felt like, "Wow you don't have to work. You could steal everything. I went to my class, saw my teacher who said that she had to talk to me. When Rosie came up to my face,she looked straight in my eyes, and said, "Jimmy, no b———t. I need the ten dollars you took." I mean she didn't even ask if I took it; she knew I took it, so I gave it to her.Now still in the third grade when it was time to get our report card, there was a lot of cheers going around the room. Kids were asking, "What class are you in." "Yeah, where in the same class." They were going into the fourth grade, and when I got my report card, my heart dropped to the floor. I felt like sh———t; I was to repeat the third grade. I felt effed up walking home and started picking on this big kid. I was a F———ng prick. Let me get some glue; maybe I'll feel better. I believe that when I turned and really didn't give a fuck if I did anything good. That was when things got from bad to worse. Besides, I never felt good in my skin; there was always something missing, and I couldn't put my finger on it. Every time I got high, I was starting to feel good. Why? Today I know why. I'll tell you why. Because it took me out of myself, and that's how I handle things—getting high and drinking made me crazy. I guess that's why the Indians called it fire water, Sometimes, I like the way I would get.I remember we were drinking, and I started to throw the garbage cans down the basement stairs. The superintendent knew who we were. I had seen this bike under the stairs, so I took it riding. When this big kid ran into me, I was holding my leg and when I saw all the blood, I started to yell, "Help me! Help me!" My brother saw me from the window and yelled, "Jimmy! Jimmy!" He almost fell out of the window. Would you believe I actually thought that you don't need to work you could steal everything?

The cops came and took me to Mother Cabrini Hospital.

My grandmother Mima died while I was there. I was saddened. It was on 164st Edgecombe Avenue in Washington Heights. I cut two veins and chipped a bone. I still have the scars, and I was there for two weeks. While in the hospital, there was this girl who was with her brother. I was trying to get the girl alone but that wouldn't happen. In my mind, I wanted to play house with her, and her brother made sure that wasn't going to happen. None of my friends came, but my brother's friends came and cheered me up. The two weeks came and went, and I was back on the block, f——ng around (like jumping from car to car) not really giving a shit. Until I went through my brother's friend's father's car, My mother was really mad. Mr. Martin said that it was not a problem and not to worry.

Once again, I got away with it. I was only eight or nine and getting away with sh——t. So I started to rob sh——t from wherever I could get it. I robbed this store on Amsterdam and got a lot of good stuff like shirts, tools, sneakers—all kinds of sh——t. The big guys would fit me through a hole in the ceiling, and I would go to the back and open the door. I was more like a chump, and whatever they said to do, I did. I remember they said, "See that old lady over there? Rob her pocket book. You know, the purse she has in her hand. So I went over to the lady, and I started talking to her. She seemed so nice. I don't remember what we talked about, but she seemed to like me. I didn't really give her any thought. I just snatched her pocketbook. The big guys grabbed it out of my hand. This girl said not to do that and to give me something. So they give me a few dollars. I think it was five. There was forty-five dollars in the purse. All those guys that I use to hang out with, one is doing life for murder. The others are dead or in jail, and the girl that got me five dollars back, I'm glad to say that she doing well now. We text each other from time to time. She lives in Florida.

Moving from 172st to uptown to 189st, I started to hang out with the bad kids. I guess like birds of the same feather, flock together. They were a bunch of us, but soon, we weren't doing kid things anymore—from stealing things from stores to robbing.I stayed with about five, and this book is dedicated to them and their families. Now I'm the new kid on the block that came up from downtown, and the guys were cool. I used to tell my friend, Fitzy, that I gave him his wings and he would say, " Yes. You should have flew away with them." We would laugh it off and start to b——t. We also had the Bev aka Beaver and Skull Sullivan and Yunity Robert; that was the crew. It was a nice move; my mom was so happy.

To be honest, I don't have many regrets because of where I am today. But if there is one thing I could change, that would be I wish I was a better son to my mother. I'm sure she sees me today. Moving up from 172st, the guys in the new neighborhood thought I was cool. They would look up to me, and the right guys were the guys like me—little devils— would hook with guys in the neighborhood. We would walk over the George Washington Bridge and go to Palisades Amusement Park in New Jersey or take the bus there if we had money; most of the time we walked. Moving From PS173 to PS 115 on a 176st Audubon, they had a tumbling team, and there was this kid Chucky. He use to flip good and always landed on his feet. Me? Well, let's just say that I tried but always landed on my back. I could really never get the hang of it. We would have the festival in the schoolyard. My friends would come and throw eggs at our team, and security would track them down until Fritzy got caught. That was the last time they did that. Deep down inside, I was kind of glad that they got f——g caught.

All the guys I hung out with were the troublemakers. We did everything and anything until we started f——g with heroin, and that would play a big role in our lives. We would buy a two-dollar bag then go back for more all the time until we started to buy bundles—fifteen bags for twenty-eight dollars. We would sniff dope and skin pop;we would sniff glue and were open to anything.

I didn't stay in 115 for long. My mom made the transfer to PS 189 and that was right across the street from where I lived. Some time went by and I started to attend PS 189, right across from the school on Amsterdam 188-189st. (I have a picture of the school). You had Belmont Park where we played basketball rind-eve-O,

Johnny-rides-the-pony, or just hanging out. This one time, I cut school and was hanging out in the park when all the kids from my class were calling me from the window. The principal came to the park and grabbed me by the hand and tried to drag me back to school when I punched him in the face and ran. That was a bad time for me. I was starting to get in trouble a lot, not only in school but all over the neighborhood. From the truant officer to the police in the thirty-fourth precinct, I was hot, and I was only twelve to thirteen. The truant officer was on my case and would wait for my mom. The officer would tell my her that I needed to go away to a home for troubled kids like Lincoln Hall or Spofford Youth House. So they arrange for me to go to court. The day came for court then they decided that it would be in my best interest if I went to Spofford.

I was kind of nervous when I went there. This one kid says to me while we were having lunch in the mess hall that his mother never made food as good as the food in there. I asked him what. He repeated it, I got up went over to him and punched him in the face. They broke it up. When we got back to the dorm Mr. Perry asked me if I wanted to fight George. I said I did, then he asked George who said he did. So we had three minutes to fight. All the guys made a circle, and George and I went at it for three minutes then they broke it up and asked if we felt better. We said we did.

We were playing football in the yard and was losing by three points. The other team went to make a pass, and I intercepted and ran for a touchdown. We won the game; everyone went crazy. All the guys put me on their shoulders and walked me around the field. I felt great. That's a time I'll never forget. I was suppose so after the game feeling that I was pissed, That was in 1968, and I was there for my fourteenth birthday.

So leaving Spofford and going back to the neighborhood felt really good and felt a little stronger on my ego. This was in '68 when Martin Luther King was assassinated. So that's how it went. My mother decided to take me to Palisades Amusement Park while we were waiting on the rollercoaster line, who do I see? Mr Perry. I said, "Mr. Perry, it's Stalikas." He sees me and said, "Wow, Jimmy. How you doing?" I introduced him to my mom and he did the same to his wife It felt really good, so we said our goodbyes and he said, "Stalikas, stay out of trouble." I said, "Not a problem, Mr Perry." Not knowing that that was the start of my criminal career. Now I think about those times, I think to myself, *Wow! I must have killed my mom with all the sh——t I did.*

While in PS 189, I would play hookie with my music right outside the window. Like I was a superstar, I'll be drinking all the liquor in the house (my mom had a lot), and I would drink til I got crazy. It gave me courage; I would go out when I'm done drinking and do a score here and there and would make money that would only renew my thoughts about working for a living. Why work when you can steal everything?

It was around 1966, I was twelve years old at the time when I started to dip and dab with heroin. I really felt good; I liked it. I was starting to do this quite often and at times I would hear my sister saying to my mother, "He's getting high, Mom." She knew how you get when your high on heroin because her boyfriend was a junkie. My mother would ask me, "Jimmy, you're not doing drugs, are you?" I would lie to her and say, "No, Ma. How could you accuse me of getting high? Maybe I drink a little but drugs? No, I would never." At times, my mother would say, "You're just like your father." She would leave me alone for a few days til something came up. Now my chippy habit was becoming more severe, I was an effing mess. I was main lining and was only fourteen. My little habit was getting stronger and stronger

I don't know how I made it to PS 143 Junior High which was on 182st Audubon, right across the street from the cop man, so now I'm in eighth grade, only thirteen or fourteen. I'm starting to get a heroin habit. As I would walk to school from my house, I would try to do a score before I got there— and this was everyday. Sometimes I did a score; sometimes I didn't. I was a mess, and at this time, I was sniffing, clue drinking, shooting drop, shooting coke, taking Methadone—the five-dollar corner biscuits when Methadone first came out—and getting involved with this TC therapeutic program in the Bronx called Sara.

Having court cases going and being in a program was helpful, but I was still getting high and doing little scores and would get busted for this and that. I did some time but not much (a lot of skid bibs), the longest I did at one time was thirteen months in Woodbourne, New York. That was alright. My number was 7447 and was release in '74 dropped off by Yankee Stadium 161 St. and walked over the 155 St. bridge up Edgecombe Avenue, right to the house. I remember as a kid, my father would take me 155 St. to the bridge, put me on his shoulders to watch the Dodgers play before they moved to LA. We moved to 189 St. I like to say that was the start of something good, but in fact, it was the start that took a toll on me—the heroin days. But what picked up was the drinking. Here I was thinking that drinking wasn't that bad, yet it's the worst of all drugs. If you think drinking is not a drug, well then you need to be educated on alcohol. It's a deadly disease. The time I got promoted to high school was in 1970. I went to George Washington High School aka GWs. I was stung out on heroin. Mainlining into my arms and hand. I still have the scars, and here I am at sixty-five. I was a mess being in GWs. The school was right around the corner; I would go to school just to sign in then leave for the day and go pull a burglary or whatever up to no good I could do. I went into this building one time, checked the doors on the way down, and this door opened. So I walked in slowly and saw this old lady lying on the couch. I started to leave as I was going out the door and started to walk down; a lady was coming up so I said thank you, but it was now a problem. Then the lady that was walking up asked if I came from her apartment. I said I did but your mother wanted me to replace a burp, so I said thanks and that it was nothing. As I passed her, she looked right at me and walked fast to her apartment. As soon as I passed her, I flew down the stairs and out the door. Wow! That was a close one. My heart was in my feet. As I got away from that area, my heart started feeling better but still shaking up. Well, the lady had seen me; I didn't take anything, so that's cool. If got busted for being there, f—— it; I was going for a long time.

I'm glad nothing happened. Now I'm getting sick. I need a shot; I'm desperate. I needed to make a score. I went into this building and up the roof and then going down the the fire escape checking windows as I head down not really giving a f—— if someone was home or if they saw me. I got to do something,

Checking windows as I'm going down, I came across a window that was open a little, but it had a gate. There seemed to be a little light on in the next window. I tried to slide the gate, but it was locked. So I opened the window halfway, grabbed the bottom of the gate and pulled it up just enough so I could get in. As I make my way into the apartment, I hear a little music. Getting into the apartment, I looked around, took some cash that was on the dresser and started to go into the next room. I heard men talking. Holy sh———t! They're home. I better get the eff out of here. This isn't my day. So I crept my way to the door. It had a f———ng police lock, and I was scared sh———t, moving the bar back and forth from one side to the next fast. God, help get out of here. I'm about to sh———t in my pants. Then as the door opened, I took flight and ran down the stairs. My heart f———ng pumping fast; I was scared sh———t. Wow! That was a close one. On to the next f———ng score. So I made my way back to the cozy corner of 184 St. Audubon; I had about twenty-two dollars, so I cop ten deuces. They were two-dollars bags, and the deuces back then were like pounds. The slang was called "smoking." Well, at least I could get straight. I also had a wake up.

This is getting effed up. I was lost and had no direction to get straight, but there was help out there. It's that I didn't want it, not even thinking the harm I was causing my mother or the danger I invited everyday. I was out there; I was a menace not giving a f—— about anything. F—— society! But I'm a good guy; I don't want to hurt anyone. That's why I like doing burglary—because no one was involved but myself. I never liked robbery. God, that's all I need to do was to kill someone. You know and if I did, I wasn't worried about getting busted and going to jail for a long time. I was more worried about how would Jesus judge me. I never asked for help because when

I did ask for something, I would usually get it. You know how the saying goes, "Watch what you pray for because you might get it."

I was only sixteen, and I found out pretty early in my criminal career that every time I did something with someone, I got busted. So my thing was apartments. There were times I would go into nice neighborhoods, pretend I'm a salesman, go to the door, check it to see if it was open or if anyone was home, then ring the bell. If it was open, I would ease my way in and take whatever I could. Wow, I'm glad I didn't get killed. If I got killed, f—— it! They're doing me a favor. That's how I felt living like this is f—— up. I just couldn't give it up. It wasn't about feeling good and having fun. It was about survival, and sometimes, I wanted to die. But if I killed myself, God wouldn't like it. I heard somewhere if you kill yourself that's one sin that's unforgiving because you go against God's plan. So I'm f———ng stuck here. F—— it! I'll do what I can.

You know when you got that mocky on your back? So things went on like that for a while: going to Riker's for a few weeks at a time, getting detoxed here and there but always going back. I could stop but I couldn't stay stopped. That was a big problem for me, so I got busted. But this time, I was on my own, so now I can't blame anyone. I was stupid; I knew they were there but did it anyway. So they saw me and yelled, "Hey, you! Hey, you!" So I took flight and started to run and ran right into security. They busted me for breaking and entrering burglar tools weapons charge.

Back at the 34 precint bullpen seeing all the cops coming in to start their shift. "Hey, Stalikas! Got you again. You're going this time." They didn't even know why I was there. They would say sh———t just to say it and laugh it off. I would yell back eff you. Then the sergeant would tell me to watch my mouth. I would sit there waiting to go to Central Booking 100 Center St.— the tombs. While in the tombs, I had seen a lot of faces I knew. I was sick and tired of being sick and tired.

My docket number was called. I went before the judge, and she asked me if I joined a program yet. I told her yes and I really wanted to stay with it. So she gave me another date to come back, and I was to get involved with the program, get a paper signed, and bring it back. I said, "Yes, Your Honor. Thank you so much." She gave me another date, and I was released on my own recognizance. Wow! Thank you, Jesus for walking with me. My mom wanted to go to Delancey St. to do some shopping since we were right there. She bought me a cool leather jacket. I never forgot it.

Now back in the neighborhood, I ran into some of my buddies. "Jimmy, lets do something." Beav said. I, being a people pleaser, said okay, not even thinking about the pain I just put my mother through and she just bought me a jacket. So I went with them; we did a little score and started the same sh—— all over. Now we were becoming more violent. Now I'm strung out weeks past since coming out of court. I went to a program and I'm trying to get better. I go back to where I got busted last time, stole the same typewriters,and hit the cash box. This time there were two security guys, and they grabbed me and called the cops. Back to the 34 precint. Booked me, put me in the bullpen, and in the morning took me to100 Centre Street—the tombs.

Back in the tombs, one of the inmates said, "Didn't you go home last week? You're back? You got to slow down, brother." I wanted to say go eff yourself, but, you know, he was right. So I tried to slow down and stop this sh———.

Now back in the street, nothing changed. Getting involved with this program, OVR. After a while, I thought it was bullsh———. My mother's friend got me a job in a restaurant downtown where you could see my tracks on my hands. My hands were like balloons. The money I was making was only for getting high. I was an effing mess This job was getting in my way. I didn't want to work. I was involved with the Narcotic Addiction Control Commission (NACC). It was big in the '70s. Everyone was copping out to the Rocky. That's what we called the Rockefeller Program. You know, I still have the box I made when I was in the mason shop. It was a great shop. Mr,Sawsmen would bring in donuts for us; we would go around the facility and do patch up work sometimes. We had a big job, then we would have our breaks.

It was good, but just like anything else I would eff that up too. We had to grout the bathroom floor, and the grout I used smelled like the glue I use to sniff when I was younger. It f——ed me up. I took the whole can back to my cell and was sniffing it. The hack Mr. Doddy opened my cell, and he said, "Come on, Jimmy." I said, "Where are we going?" He said, "Disneyland." Right to the bin for ten days and three months on top of my time. Another time I was in the mess hall, and this guy asked me to pass the salt. So I passed it, and it fell over. The guy said that one of these days the kid is going get his teeth knock out. And I asked, "By who? You?" This guy was a big guy when he stood up. So I got up, and he got up. We went at it; he knocked me to the floor. Then he pick up the bench was about to throw it on me when my friend Sammy, Little Hercules, knocked him to the floor. It was an effing mess. It almost started a riot. I was back to the friggin' bin another three months on top of my time. I'm never getting out of this f——ng place.

As I'm writing this, I think about some of the guys I used to hang out with. This one guy, Tommy, he wanted to hook me up with his sister when we got out. I left in July of '74; he was getting out in August of '74. I called him and a lady said, "Tommy is no longer with us." I'm thinking maybe I didn't hear that right, so I called again. I said, "Hello. I'm looking for Tommy. He just got home from the program. Can I speak to him?" The lady on the phone said, "Are you one of Tommy's friends? I said that I was. She said, "Tommy went right back to getting high, and he OD yesterday." I said, "Who am I talking to?" She said she was his mother, and I said, "Excuse me. I'm so sorry." We talked a little then hung up. I felt f——ed up.

I heard of another kid that passed. He was with us, and he was just twenty-two. I'm telling you it doesn't care how old you are, what color you are, what gender—it robs you of life. That was in '74. Today I hold all my batteries in a box I made while in the mason shop. I'm sure the program helped a lot of guys. That's like doing a bid. You go away in a facility. It's like jail, then you get on aftercare, which is like parole. You're assigned an aftercare officer. I wasn't ready; I was doing all kinds of sh—— robbing apartments, bikes, cars, churches, whatever I could, I did. I was a f——ng mess. Maybe I'll just jump off the effing roof; it would be over in a minute. That thought was wiped out when I thought that wouldn't be right by my God. I don't think he'll like that, so that thought I had was gone. If I would have thought those thoughts before doing them, chances are I wouldn't have done none of the stuff I did.

It was time for court. They sent me back, so back to the block. When is this friggin' vicious cycle going to friggin' end. Now here I go again. This was in 1974; my number was 7447 // 210 Criminal Commitment one day to five years. We were still living in the heights. Mom decided to move to COOP City in the Bronx. The move went well. So after working as a busboy in this fancy restaurant, we moved to Coop City where we had three bedrooms and two baths. It was a beautiful apartment overlooking the New York garbage dump. My friend Beaver was always saying what a nice view of the dump, so I just laughed it off and just went along with it. I was working here and there, nothing steady, a few weeks. I didn't go back to shooting dope but my drinking picked up.

The '70s were here; disco fever was on the rise. A movie called *Saturday Night Fever* was out, and I was bouncing around from one club to the next. I was blowing coke here and there; no needles anymore, just drinking and partying. Good girls were never a problem for me. I love them and leave them. To me, they're all the same (You know like the song goes). No hard drugging but always looking to make a score. This time it would be stickups. I would take off whatever I needed to do at the time, no planning. I just did stuff, and drinking gave me the courage to think I was King Kong. This behavior stayed with me for years. Thank God nobody got killed. There are times today I pass by places where I did a score; I think about the harm and grief I caused people and feel bad sometimes. I wondered why I'm still here. When I was driving a cab, a passenger told me, "God, I not only see the present but I also see the future." I'm sure he has his reasons for being here.

I think about my man, Beaver; he was two years younger than me. His father use to coach baseball when we were kids when we were doing fun things like kids do. But some time passed, and we were criminals—junkies, thieves, robbers. I was like a zombie, and my mother would call me the walking zombie—I would be cleaning the house at two to three in the morning. I remember one night, after shooting dope, I looked in the mirror, and I was all yellow. I believe that was the time I contracted hepatitis C, a blood disease that stayed with me for many years. I would try and sell a pint of blood to this blood bank, and after looking at me, they said, "No, thanks. We have enough."

Everyone and their mothers were getting high, except my mom. There was no more real fun; we were drinking, sniffing glue, shooting dope, taking whatever we could take to get us out of ourselves. Nothing big. You could take me out of Washington Heights, but you can't take Washington Heights out of me. I got a kick out of these people trying to make a musical out of Washington Heights when I know, for me, it was more like a cesspool of insanity. When I told my brother, he would always say that me and my crowd were like zombies. He said to me one time, "Jimmy, Washington Heights was a great neighborhood. Many famous people came from there. Calling it a place of insanity, that's because everyone you know were junkies and robbers." He has a point there.

Now I'm in the Bronx, living in Coop City. From where I lived in section 5, I could walk to Pelham Bay, catch the six train or the express to the city across the highway going into Pelham Bay. My dancing and drinking picked up. It was late mother got home late because she works late nights at Columbia Presby Medical Center. That's cool if I take her car; I will be back early. Then she can go to work. She had a 1972 pinto, so one night I decided to take the car and started to head downtown, like I got somewhere. So three days had passed since I took the car, and my mother knows I would always call her. She thought something must be wrong. She told my sister Rose that I wasn't home for three days, and she doesn't have her car. She decided to report the car stolen. When she got a call from the police department, they told her the car was in an accident. Then she asked what happened to the driver. They told her the driver was in critical condition. The night before that, my sister Rosie had a dream about Fort Washington Avenue. She couldn't make out the dream, but when my mother got a call from the police department, then she asked what hospital was he in. They told her that he's in Columbia Presby on the Fort Washington Avenue and that is where special trauma cases go. She said thanked them and hung up. Wow! That's where my mother worked. I could feel her pain now; how she must of felt not knowing what condition I was in but knowing that it was critical. When she came into where I was, she said there were tubes all over me—in my mouth, nose, and in my arms. For three weeks, she told me my friends—Fitzy, Beaver, Robert, and a few others—came all the time to try and get me going. They would tell the doctor that I was responding to them. The doctor would say that it was impossible since I was in a coma. After three weeks of visits, I woke up to my mother and sister saying to my sister Angela that I saw Daddy. Daddy came to see me, and my sister would say, "Don't you remember, Jimmy? You found Daddy dead last month on your birthday." I didn't even know how old I was. Everyone was excited that I woke up. My mother cried; Anglea was happy. The next day all my friends showed up.

The next day, going to Helen Hayes Rehab was a life saver. The staff was great. Going into rehab, I stayed there for two months; while I was there, I had seen a lot of heartache stories. I guess you could say that accident was a blessing in disguise. My blood was infected with aal. When my family would come, my niece Rosie wanted to race me in the yard. So I said, "Sure. On your mark, get ready, and go." My niece took off, and I couldn't even move, thinking I could run. We laughed the way I tried to run. Forget about it; I was stiff and having this deadly disease VD—what a shameful disease—yet a curable one. Eight shots of penicillin and you're good to go.

After some time while in the hospital, I was able to go home, yet I wasn't all that right. My brains were still scrambled while in the hospital. The doctors wanted me to give them a list of all the girls I was active with. I knew why they wanted it, and I gave them some bullshit info, at least I still had the sense of being aware why they wanted that information. So now I'm home and my emotions were off. I used to tell people that if they had an accident and they had their seatbelt on, they probably would get killed. Seatbelts are bad. You see I had it all backwards. I had no sense of embarrassment. It took a while for me to somewhat get right in the head. I was working down Canal Street in this packing company, and the boss would lock me in from eight in the morning to three in the afternoon and told me to bring my lunch. So one day after leaving the packing job, I walked by this building under construction. It was 369 Canal Street right off of West Broadway, so I went on to the job, asked a few guys if they needed help. They pointed to this man, so I went over to him and asked if he needed help. He asked if I ever worked construction before; I lied and said I did. He said come tomorrow at seven in the morning and give it a try.

The next day he gave me a job making ten dollars an hour. I said it was cool. So after leaving the packing job, I went back and told the boss I won't be coming back. I bought the boss a card and thanked him. I told him that I wouldn't be coming back and then said goodbye.

Working with the construction crew was good. I had a lot of good guys and was working for about four months. So while working one day, I needed to take ten full lengths 2x4 studs up to the ninth floor but the freight was on the tenth floor. I was ringing the bell, but it wasn't coming down, so I walked all the way up to the tenth floor and expecting to see no one there. Who do I see? Carlos the plumber turning pipe. So I said, "Carlos, you couldn't send the Elevator down." He said, "Motherf—er I didn't hear it." "I was ringing it for ten minutes, and don't be calling me a motherf—er." I said "F—ck you." So he came running down the ladder to kick my ass, and he had the two-foot wrench in his hand. He started swinging when I blocked his swing. He grabbed me, and we started to fight. Guys from downstairs came up and broke it up. This big Jamaican guy, John, had me up against the studs and kept saying, "No, Jimmy. Fighting no good," as he blocked me. Carlos the plumber came around and sucker punched me in the nose. I started to bleed, went downstairs got cleaned up, came back to the floor where Carlos was, and said, "Carlos, we'll take care of this problem across the street in the dumps, lunch time." He said, "No, motherf—er. Now." He came off the ladder, and we started to fight. Carlos then came around and sucker punched me in the nose when I started to bleed. "John get the f— off from blocking me." So I went down to get cleaned up came back up to the floor where carlos was, I seen him and said Carlos lunch time where take care of this problem lunch time across I the street in the dumps and he said No Now MFER He had his two foot wrench in his hand; he went and he took a swing at me. I blocked it and punched him in the nose. He hit the wall. I kept punching him, then a rush of blood spread over the wall. The guys from upstairs came downstairs. The guys from downstairs came up. Mr,C came and ask what did I hit him with? "Mr.C, he hit the wall when I punched him. He came at me with the wrench, Mr.C." Then he said, "Go home. Go out the back way like a real f—ng gangster." So I left, getting home walking towards my building in Coop City 26C, Pelham Bay last stop on the six train that was like a pussy train. The girls on the six train were hot and had no problem getting their number. I met this other girl on the six train and one of the clubs I used to go to and dance. I knew all the waitresses, and this one waitress wanted me to go over her house and cut her hair for ten dollars. I said sure. So we made plans the day, and while I was cutting her hair, her daughter came home, and she introduced me to her. She said, "I know Jimmy from the six train" The mother looked at me surprisingly. Then a few minutes later, her other daughter came home, and I knew her from the six train. The mother said, "You know everyone on the six train." We started to laugh. Her mother said, "What? You talk to everyone on the six train?" We laughed some more, and she gave me fifteen bucks. I said my goodbyes. Getting to Pelham Bay, I would walk towards the tracks, cross the tracks, and there is 26C. Then I'm home. There were two detectives walking towards me, and they said, "Stalikas." I said, "Who wants to know?" He said, "My name is Detective Vigilante,

from the First Precint down Hudson Street. I understand you had a fight with a plumber on the job from New York Construction. I said, "I did." He said, "He's in a coma. If he dies, that's going to be another issue. I want you to call me every day at one in the afternoon, okay?

Until this is resolved the right way. I said, "Sure. Thank you." So he gave me his card. So I started to call him thinking about when I was in the coma from the car accident. Now this guy is in a coma from a fight. Wow, that sucks, and sh—t if he dies. I'm really screwed. I'm looking at time, and it's not gonna be ninety days. Wow, from a fight on the job, I'm looking at a serious problem here. I was praying and praying: God, let this be alright. Help Carlos recover. I couldn't do anything but wait to see how this worked out. Mr.C didn't want to be bothered with me; I set him back big time. My mother was very scared. So after three weeks, he said I didn't have to call him anymore. He came out of the coma. He'll be alright.

Wow! God, thank you.

I think about that today, and I believe at the time I wanted to kill him. I felt really bad that this guy treated me like that, coming at me with a wrench, and I was the only one on the job that talked to this guy. Nobody liked him; he was always alone. I was a friend to him, and he laughed and punched me in the face while I blocked him. Now that wasn't right.

Today I think something good came out of what Mr. C told me to take some time off and after two weeks to give him a call. So I called after two weeks can back to work but was driving the van bringing materials to the other jobs, and when I went to the other jobs, all the guys would say, "There's Jimmy," and would come to me talk. The bosses didn't like that, so after a little while of doing that Mr. C said, "Jimmy, we're slowing down. Won't be needing you anymore." So that's that for that. So now I was out of work, my brains were still scrambled; I was a mess. Living in Coop would be still scrambled. Then I would go to the city at the time in the '70s. There was sh—t to do but no car. Living in Coop, I met a few local girls and started to hang out with them and after a while, there wasn't that much to do unlike today. I went to this neighborhood bar and hanging out, listening to music, dancing had a good time. I met some girls. This was in 1975 Girls, booze, drugs, and rock 'n' roll. I slowed down on crime, did a few scores here and there—nothing big to talk about.

Being into carpentry, I decided to build my mother a closet for her in the spare room. Remember my brains are still scrambled from the accident. So I went to this lumber yard ordered some wood. They sold me the most expensive wood; I had it delivered. I started to feel people were taking advantage of me because I didn't have any sense. I had things backwards, like when I was in the hospital—Helen Hayes Rehab—thinking positive was good. When I was tested for VD, they said I was positive, and I would tell people I'm positive, thinking it was good. When a nurse said, "Jimmy, positive is bad. It's negative that is good." So I stepped back. Yeah, I got things backward alright. That's scary twenty-two. Why should I give a f—ck?

Friends scattered. Beaver was working with the horses. He was doing good. I would go to the stables with him in Yonkers Raceway. He would tell me that the security guard yelled at him one time saying, "Get out of here." We would laugh it off. He would say we're not junkies no more; we're alcoholics. He was right. I did more serious sh—t when I was stung out on dope, and it would be many years before I realize that. I don't have many regrets, but I do wish he was still around knowing what I know today about drugs and alcohol. I'm sure he would have gotten sober. He was driving for this this messager company. He damaged the company car. He had a fight with his girlfriend, and he was home alone drinking all day. He decided to kill himself. After a few days, his brother in-law decided to go to his apartment to see if he was home. He was hanging from the bathroom door; he hung himself. We had no cellphones back then, and when I finally found out about it, and it had been five days, and at the time, I was working for an inspection Company—Inspection Concrete in Woodlawn Cemetery. I was working and bumming change from a labor to get a drink. I checked my log, and I was working when my best friend was being buried. I didn't even know he died. When I finally got a hold of his sister, I asked her why didn't get a hold of me. She said they were looking for me, and they couldn't find me. Sh—t, how bad I felt. That started to play a big deal in my life—getting mad at this f—ng alcohol. It robs you of everything—your family, friends. It takes everything, and it lies to you. It tells you, "I piece of sh—t nobody likes you or loves you; you might as well take a dive off the f———ng roof like my ex-wife's friend did, and he just had a baby girl or like my friend, Tom, drowned off the rocks, drinking. He hit his head and died. Man, how f———ng Mad I got with this f———ng drugs & alcohol. Tipping over on the Westside Highway, getting thrown from the car fifty feet, I was given my last rights by a priest. Then three weeks later, I wake up to my sister and mother, saying "Daddy came to see me," and my sister Angela said, "You know, Jimmy, you found Daddy dead last month on your birthday." My birthday! I didn't even know how old I was.

This alcohol has got to go. It doesn't care what color you are, how old you are, or what sex it—takes all of you. Man, it was a blessing when I ran into this pretty girl. She told me that she thinks I might have a drinking problem.I said, "Me? Nah, I stopped shooting dope. I could stop anything." She said that it's not about stopping drinking; it's about staying stopped. That resonated with me; she made sense. I'm saddened to mention the girl that I was in love with who told me about where I could change my life and never have to drink or do drugs again is know longer with us. She OD'd.

One day as I was looking for my father in St. Raymond's Cemetery, I came across the girl and her mother's tombstone. I heard after Kathy died, her mother lost it, and she died soon after. I said a few words and continued to look for my dad. I went to see my father for my birthday and found him dead; alcohol took him. He drank himself to death. I could stop, but I couldn't stay stopped. Thinking about what my man said, "We're not junkies no more but we're alcoholics."

So some time went by and I decided I needed a different career, Saw the movie, *Shampoo*, and decided that's what I wanted to do—to be a hairstylist and be around girls all the time. So I went to Bronx Beauty School, had an instructor that was on my case a lot. She didn't like the fact that her son and I would talk sometimes about going to the bar right next to the school. We would stay there a few hours, and that drove the instructor crazy. That had to stop, and it did after a little while. I had a date with one of the prettiest girls in the school. Before he died, Beaver and I were going to double date, and when I was a few minutes late, I found my metal. I gave her on the step, and she stood us up thinking we stood her up. Now that was effed up; she couldn't wait ten minutes. When I went back to school, she switch to nights. Eff her. It would be a while before I ran into her again. F—k it that was my attitude. When I was in school, I was hanging out in the bar next to the school with the son of the instructor more. She didn't like that. This was in October of '76.

My mother died from cancer. Wow! I had no job, drinking, blowing coke. I wasn't a junkie, but my life was unmanageable. It would be a while before I sobered up.

That's how sh—t went for a while. All effed up, but not looking at my drinking, construction was slow. The school was in the Castle Hill section of the Bronx, so I would go from section five to Pelham Bay catch the six train, go a few stops, and I'm there. I met a few girls there and started seeing this one girl. I was hanging out with her at my house, met her uncle, and at time my mother was sick. So one day, I saw my mom crying. I said, "Ma, what's the problem?" She said that she hopes to live long enough to see that I'll be alright. I grabbed her and hugged her and said, "May God forbid something does happen to you. I'll always be alright." In about four weeks after that, my mom died. My oldest sister made it clear to me, "Jimmy, you can't stay with us." My other sister and brother were in Florida, so I decided to let the equity for the Coop run out, then I got a one-bedroom in the Westchester Square in the Bronx area where all I did was drive and drink in the cab and getting high. But I wasn't putting a needle in my arm; I was still f—ck up, getting high when I can. That was a blessing when I met that girl in the diner. The seed was planted; she steered me on a road that would change my life. I started looking at myself; it was great living in a furnished room. Walking to the meeting.

I was driving a cab but not making much. I didn't really care about money. Money was never an issue for me—I had it; I didn't have it. It was never a problem for me, but when I was strung out, it was a big issue.

Things kept on going from one crisis to the next. Maybe I'll get killed, and there were times when I came close to getting hit many times. I guess you could call it the luck of the alcoholic. F—ck it! That was cool too. I started dating a lot; I was like a male whore, clubbing, leaving with this one or that one. The girl that introduced me to the program…well, we know what happened to her. It's sad, but God has a plan. If I don't take a swan dive off a roof or take a hot shot maybe you achieve your purpose. It wasn't easy, purpose.

How could I achieve my purpose when I don't even know what it is? I have to go back to when I was in the coma of how I felt and thought of my existence. Yes, do I have a purpose? It's in his plan, not ours. When we hang ourselves or take a swan dive off of the roof or put a pistol in our mouth and pull the trigger, we make that choice which disrupts God's plan.

Washington Heights is a cesspool of insanity, where everyone and their mothers were getting high. But my mother, to be honest, I don't know how I got out of the '70s in one piece is beyond me. In and out of jail programs kept reminding me how effed up I was. I wasn't getting in trouble any more since we move to the Bronx. I was driving for this cab company in the Bronx. I would be drinking and driving. No more dope, but I was doing anything and everything from pills to blowing coke and to doing a score here and there, thinking as long as I don't shoot dope, I'll be alright. That was the most stupid idea I ever had. In fact, it was worse, and I did more severe crimes in the Bronx then I did when I was strung out on junk. Wow, I get busted for this shit. What's my excuse now? You're not putting a needle in your arm, yet you're still a f——ng nut still doing bad things. The help that came to me was never late but always on time. After the problem that happen in the Westchester Square area in the Bronx, I met this girl. She moved into the furnace room with me; she fixed it up and made it look like something. A friend of ours was moving and asked me if I like to take over his apartment. I was working on my ninety and ninety, you know, going to meetings in ninety days (We call it the 90/90). I have gotten a sponsor but wasn't really making an effort. My sponsor would call and he'll say that we're going to a meeting. I would ask what time. It's like it was no big deal. I always go back to if I stop shooting drop. I could stop anything. My problem was that I couldn't stay stopped. My wife's friend came over the house to install phone jacks for a few dollars, so when he came, he asked if he could light up a joint. Instead of saying no and that I'm trying to stay sober, I said, "Sure, no problem." People pleasing again, and I'm the one that pays the price. He lit it up, took a poke, and passed it to me; like an alcoholic, I took it. Wow, I f—cked up again. I heard some say that you can't be high and sober at the same time, and my wife ask what am I going do. Definitely, going to talk to my sponsor. So as I go over to his house and he said to me, "God, good. I need someone to give me a hand covering my pool. And Jimmy you're ready." I said, "I was, and it has been thirty-seven years on December twelve." Then he said, "Hold on to your seat." He wasn't lying. "Going tonight, want to go?" I said, "Sure," and today I'm still going.

I wasn't ready so I shared it, and this time I wanted to do this right thing. No more shortcuts. I got to take the suggestions, like my sponsor would say, "Take the suggestions like you betters. If you don't, you're playing with them, and your pay the price." At this time I was in a program and working it. I was working with a friend that's also in the program; we were working in Connecticut. My wife said to me, "You're gonna start all over. What about Joey, your sponsor? What you gonna do?" I said, "We'll see," and went to work. That was on my eighty-ninth day. My friend went to congratulate me on my ninety and ninety. I said, "Thanks but I messed up. I took a drag out of a joint yesterday, and I'm gonna do another ninety and ninety." He said, "At least you're getting honest." When he said that I felt the gates of heaven didn't open up, but the gates of hell sure did.

That was thirty-seven years ago, so the road to recovery wasn't easy. Like we say in the rooms, my worst day sober is much better than my best day drinking. In my case, drinking or drugging to me were the same. Anything that takes me out of myself is deadly. The day came when I made my ninety and ninety, and right after that, my sponsor suggested that it was time I go out speaking. So going out speaking was cool. I got more back then I shared. A friend that I knew would ask me to speak at her first anniversary, and I said I would. So as I was sharing, I would say that on my eighty-ninth day,

I took a drag out of a joint. It was suggested that I do another ninety and ninety. After I shared at the anniversary, she came to me and said that I did a great job. It bothered her that I said that I took a drag out of a joint because she smoked a whole joint. I asked, "Did you tell your sponsor about that?" She said that she did, so I asked what the sponsor say. She said not to do it anymore. So I said that I think she should get another sponsor.

Day one begins today. It might seem tough, but that's how we do it. You can't be high and sober at the same time, and when you don't think this is serious and follow the suggestions the way it's suggested, like you pick up a drug or drink in your sobriety, you start over just like when I had eighty nine days. I wasn't worried about starting my time over because I know all I have is today, and that's why the suggestions are like you are better than me. Like my sponsor Joey said, you take the suggestion as you betters because if you don't, your play with it. You know, he was right. After a while, I heard that she got killed by her boyfriend. Always remember that suggestion as you betters to me.

You know one thing that I'm so grateful for is having a good sponsor that tells me like it is, just like when he told me that to this day that's what I do, and I got to remember I'm only an arm's length away from a drink or drug. I'm going towards a drink or away from a drink. Sobriety is good. Even with all that knowledge, I had to test the waters again. Thinking that not wanting to drink and do drugs isn't enough. You have to take action. Even knowing that invisible line is always there waiting in the cuff for you to mess up.

As I was driving steady, we said, "Sure." We took the apartment over. I always wanted to make my confirmation. I made my communion when I was eight. I always wanted to make my confirmation and at the age of thirty-five, I made my confirmation. I wasn't making that many meetings. I had my mother-in-law come over; we had like a little party being that I made my confirmation. I asked my sisters to come; they didn't. They probably thought that is was no big deal. It's not like I'm a kid who just made his confirmation. Even though I was up there in age, I still thought that would have been nice for my family to come but they didn't. What am I expecting too much from my family? Maybe.

But as time goes by, my mother-in-law left the big bottle of half full wine in the house one day. I took a little and a little and before I knew it, I was effed up. My wife came home with blow, took that, and went to the bar down the street from me seen this bartender I knew and started slapping his face like, "Hey buddy. How you doing?" Someone walked by and punched me in the face. I went home, changed my clothes, grabbed a hammer, and went to the bar. As I cut the corner so quick, there were cops all over. I didn't even know cops own that bar. God, if they seen the hammer in my hand, it's all over,

As I enter the packed bar, there was no one in the bar. All the people outside were cops. I knew the bartender and he knew me so getting punched in the face and thrown out, I guess he knew I'll be back. I mean how long did It take to come back? Less than ten minutes? Not a soul was in the bar when I went in. Entering the bar with a hammer in my hand, I could see one cop creeping behind me another coming in at the front, another coming in through the door. Thinking to myself, *I'm f—cked*. I knew they were about to grab me, so I played with that. Let them take me down. So one cop grabbed me, threw me to the floor. The other cops were f——ng me up, took me to Jacobi Hospital. I was loud, so they took me to the 48 precint on the CB, The Cross Bronx, and wow, now I really f—cked one of the cops that was trying to punch my face into the floor.He broke his hand. They had me for a slew of things. My knees felt like they were crack, blood dripping down my face, thrown in a roach-infested cell This is bad. I fell asleep in my cell for about fifteen minutes and when I woke up, I was feeling great. I had a vision that things will be okay when was another story. I'm in deep sh—t now. One cop said, "Hey, you no stranger to jail and crime, huh?" "That was a while ago. I'm trying do the right thing." The cop says, "Yeah? By going after someone with a hammer?"Yeah, he had a point. I'm sick of this sh—t. I'm not a junkie anymore. I'm worse, and I'm an alcoholic, not even putting a needle in my arm. God, help me get out of here; I'll try again. At this time in my life, I'm facing jail time, facing felony charges that I didn't get when I was bad and when I was a junkie. Now I get them. That effing alcohol really sucks. I'm telling you that alcohol really lies to you. It is pure evil—the devil's tools. It takes as many lives as it can with no regard for sex or race. It's the devil that's makes you feel like a star and invincible. That effng alcohol. When in front of the judge as she was turning my record, my sister said her face got more and more angry. They wanted to give me one to four in Elmira. I was about thirty and decided that I had enough. I was thinking about taking the one to four. Then my lawyer said that he'll get me five years probation.So I copped out to E felony five-years probation. Sister Angela bailed me out. I had to go back for sentencing. I know I can't drink, and I can't stop for the rest of my life, but I could stop for today.So after getting out, I decided to pass by my sponsor's house and talk to him. So as I was passing by, he said, "Hey, are you hurting enough this time?" I said, "What are you talking about?" He said, "Are you tired of being sick and tired? I said, "Yes, I am." He said, "Knowing that you don't want to drink and do drug in your case no more isn't enough. You have to learn go back to meeting and take it a day at a time." Wow, how much better I feel by just talking to him. That's how they do it. They take it a day at a time.

I get released, go back to the meeting, and I start to listen. I heard so much good stuff, and they talk about a tool box. When you hear something, you like hold on to it, and put it in your tool box because you never know when you're going to use it. Some time went by. Wow, I'm coming up on a year. In the last year, I've been sober making meetings. My brother-in-'s father hooked me up with the construction union with good pay and good benefits. This isn't like what I'm used to This is where you retire from. I needed the bennies; my wife is having a baby. Some time went by, she had the baby. It's a boy, so we named it James. After a short while, she was pregnant. She said to me, "I can't see why people have more than one kid." I asked her why did say that? She said that it's like your lip being pulled over your head. So we didn't have the baby. I really didn't want to do it. I felt effed up but went along with it (like a chump). I know it's their body. It really sucks when you have no control over doing anything about it. Today I feel alright about it because my son Is alright with it.

I remember I went to a party when I had about six months in, and it was a sober dance. I didn't feel good; I felt nervous and scared a little. I wanted to get high, but I remember someone saying that if you feel nervous or scared, call someone. So I did. We didn't have cells back then. I didn't bother looking for a phone, so I just left. They say your second year could be tough for you, So I ask, why do you say that? He said something like, "'Cause you feel good. You're sober and yet, you're not feeling that good 'cause you feel something is missing." I could understand that but I couldn't put my finger on it. My situation when I celebrated two years was less active than when I had celebrated one year. I had one year and saying to myself, *I got this*. Yeah right ! When I hear guys going back out there after ten years, it's always because they slack up on meetings, So I better get back in the swing of things and start banking more meetings myself. Coming up on five years,what five years? I got to be crazy. I think about how I did it. Wow, a day at a time!

Someone once told me, yesterday's a memory and tomorrow a mystery and today my reality.

I like that. Sounds sensible to me. In fact, all I have been hearing for the last five years sounds good. Wow, I could do this. I'm gonna stay on course. Around this time, my wife is taking a serious look at her drinking. We talk but you know I stop feeling for her as a husband. She wasn't really making me feel whole. So she started making meetings, asking me questions which I thought was good. We would share a bit feel good for a while and back to the disagreements at the same time making family functions work with the union. When I wasn't working with construction, I always got busy with other things. With a clear head, I could say that it's been good. My son is five years old now and in school, and he likes it. Nothing exciting in the marriage but acting as if we are happy. My wife came home one day and said to me, "You can't even seem to be happy to see me when I come home?" I was speechless; it just wasn't there. I could remember when she said that. I felt bad for my son. So we started to go to a marriage counselor but at one hundred twenty-five dollars and hour per visit? After three visits, she was really not saying much as the money was getting tight, and I just stopped going. We sat dormant for a few years bringing our son up. He was about eight when she decided to separate from me, and it's not that I blame her. It's just what she wanted. Still making meetings, I was coming up on ten years; she was coming up on five. I still can't believe I have been sober for ten years. It's beyond me. Even with ten years, things weren't that good. Not working much, living in Westchester. Well, at least my son is in a good school district. She came home one day and said she had something to tell us. So we sat down with my son and she said that she found an apt in town. *Wow, look at this sh—t*, thinking to myself. *I spent close to ten years with this b—tch now she wants to move.* So I asked, like a good man, when was she leaving and that I'll help her move. So with the help from some great guys, we moved her when she wanted it. We moved her in town. I would see my son often; I had no problems with that. I was driving an old car, missing time at work trying to get something going. Things were just effed up. But one good thing, I was sober, and that's all that mattered.

After we separated, I was always in touch with my son. I would go to his hockey games and we would go to the movies and then go out for pizza. We would have a good day then I would bring him home. He would ask me, "Dad, where you going from here?" I would say," Going out dancing." "Okay. Be careful," he would say.

While I was out one night, I met this nice looking girl while dancing. We danced together. So we started dating; she had two boys. We exchanged numbers. After a few calls, we started to date, and she became my girlfriend for five years—five long F——ng years. Around this time, I slowed up on the dancing as I became just a helper. I spent a lot of money moving her and her sons to a much better area from the Bronx. So I had to get out of this f———ng relationship. Her ex would come around at times and say he was going to give her some money. She would always return pissed. He didn't give her anything; maybe it's because I was there.

So after moving her and her sons to Westchester, we lived in a nice area, and I was working construction for the union. She worked in White Plains; it was convenient. One of her sons would say, "You know, Mommy has a boyfriend." We haven't been intimate for a while, so she came home one day and left early like she had to go somewhere. Right then and there, I knew I needed to end this. I was working nights; the job was tough. I made it home late one day; I was tired and her son was banging on the door. So I went downstairs to see who was the asshole banging on the door, and it was her son, the one that always gave me a problem. So I left after a few effed up words. I said, "F—ck this." and moved out. I found an apartment quick, not to mention my dog got killed when she let him out the house. Here I am coming from work late because I was buying her dog dogfood, and she puts my dog out. I just missed my dog by minutes. I saw her outside calling Rocket, so I asked why she was calling for Rocket. She said it was because she had just put her out. I asked, "Why did you put him out? She's in the basement and not bothering anyone." (She was pissing; that's why she's in the basement.) She said, "'Cause she was pissing." "But she's in the basement where she goes. Why did you have to put him out and how long were you calling her?" She said, "Five minutes." So I take her sons bike and start looking for my dog. I start calling out, Rocket, Rocket. As I was riding, a girl pulls up to me and ask if I'm looking for a small dog. I say I am. She says that she had seen a dog by 9A and that he might have gotten hit by a car. So I pedal fast calling out for Rocket. As I came up on an overpass, there was a hump on the road. It was Rocket. She just got hit by a car. So feeling sad, a lady pulled up, and I asked her to help, which she did. The girl who told me where my dog might have gotten hit by a car pulled up and said, "Here, I got the right size box." I put Rocket in the box and her son said, "What? You got Rocket in there? I said suddenly, "I did." Going back to the house, she puts my dog out, and she gets it killed.

But you know as much as I hate that b—tch, something good came out of it. I found a new talent within me—writing. I remember in one of the passengers It says, The house of Misery. And you know it was the house of misery. She reads it, and says this is the house of misery. You know I was the type of guy that wanted to do the right thing; her husband cheated on her, so she went and cheated on me. At least I'm free from that two-timing b—tch.

Making a meeting, I must say this: Being with that girl, I never mentioned her in the rooms. Why I'll tell? Because it was all about sex, and I know they would have said it wasn't a good relationship. She would say from time to time like what's going happen to us. I'll tell you: You cheated on me that's what happened. There was a time in the relationship that I was going do something, and it was a permanent solution to a temporary problem. Thank God, I didn't go through with it If I would have, I would have been one sorry soul.

Moving into Deerhaunt Drive in Croton-on-Hudson, whatelse could I say? I tried. She did tell me she didn't think it was a good idea us living together after the house of misery. The move was the best thing I did for myself. Living in Westchester was nice. I was in this group, and it snowed heavy the night before. When I got to the meeting no one was there, and the snow was like two feet high. Then this guy came, then another. They wanted to call the meeting off. I said, "No, we don't call the meeting. Snow didn't stop you from drinking or drugging, did it?" He said, "No." So we grabbed some shovels and started to make a path. When we were done we had about twenty people show up, and it was a good meeting.

We are only trusted servants; no one governs. It's good to have time; it's that you heard the message more. Whoever got up earlier that's what counts. I like that idea. Their way,not my way. I stayed with that for a while. I'm changing despite myself; my unspoken prayers are answered. I am among most men so richly blessed. If I say anything that's nice, it's because I learned it here. As time goes by, I'm living with this girl that I married because she was pregnant, and I wanted her under my coverage with the union. I thought at the time that I loved her. After a while, she was due, and I was right there all the way til I saw my son. He looked so strong. I was so happy, a feeling of joy busted out of me, like wow I'm a father now. No more F——ng around. So being a union man, I felt good making meeting, going out speaking, being a dad and husband. Going out speaking was great. You get so much back. Now this is the name of the game. I heard in the rooms somewhere when you go to a meeting, don't forget to grab the gold coin on the way out because if you get enough gold coins maybe you could buy your life back. You can't really weigh the benefits you get from working the program compared to your drinking days. It outweighs the drinking days by far. Yeah, you have bad moments but bad days? Nah, I'l tell you a lot of weight was lifted off my shoulders when I accepted the fact is: that's all I have is today. You know what's scary? It only takes a minute for you to F—ck up. We call them invisible lines; I pass through them a few times. I have to remember nobody is going take care of me. I got to watch my own back. When I think of going to the old neighborhood and letting everyone see how good I'm doing, I'm setting myself up for a fall. Nobody cares. They rather see you looking like sh—t, feeling bad, and homeless then to see you doing good with money in your pocket and driving a nice car. Misery does love company. That's where we say this is a selfless program for complicated people. We take our sobriety very seriously. I'll tell you time does go by so fast, We can't take anything for granted. December twelve, I would be thirty-seven years. Wow, I remember when I had thirty in the program and still shoot someone in the face with a BB gun when he started to bleed from the mouth. I'll tell you, you're only an arm's length away from a drink. Things are changing all the time; you only have now! When he called the cops on me, what happened was it seemed like the music was loud. He lived next door to me; he was in his thirties. So I went to the backyard to ask him to lower the music, and I couldn't reach the door because there was a fence in the way of about six feet. So I started to hit his door with a mop handle. He opened the door and says a few choice words to me, which I did not like. Then he spat at me and calls me a mother effer. Up on the fence I went, punched him in the head, went inside and got my BB gun. He says, "What are you gonna do with that?" and he went to spit at me again. I shoot him in the face and he started to bleed from the mouth. He ran inside. In that moment I knew I was F—cked0, so I grabbed my dog, took the gun, and started to leave. I ran upstairs, hid the gun, and went to leave. He was outside waiting for the cops. As I went out, he jumped on me at the same time the cops came and arrested me. My neighbor took care of the dog. Now I'm locked the eff up with thirty years of sobriety. The last time I was in jail was thirty years ago where I had assault charge on the police E Felony for that. After the judge's face was getting more angry as she was turning the pages. Sh—t, it seemed like after thirty years, nothing changed. It seemed years ago like it didn't mean anything. I laid up on the boat; it's a brother to Rikers Island.

For about two weeks, it seemed like nothing changed—got right into jailing again. This Boat that I was on is in the Huntspoint area in the Bronx. I never heard of it before. It's a prison on a barge that was in Louisiana ship. Up here, it was a federal prison, and it was no country club. To me, jail is jail. It was no joke; it was just as bad as the rock. Riker's maybe worst. One morning, one of the guard asked me for my password to my bank card that my son needed. Within a week, I was bailed out.

I had this legal aide. She was good. She was telling me they wanted to give me a year in jail time. My lawyer said no way. Thirty years without an arrest, no I am not going to jail. Felt good when she said that. So they kept postponing it. I copped out to another E Felony and got another five years probation and take anger management which I did. Basically what they do is just point out your anger and as you recognize your anger, it gives you a moment to think about your reaction. Then what? If I thought about my reaction to my anger, then I would've done a lot of sh—t I did. I guess I should have listened to my inner voice. So I did that for eight months while on bail. After two and a half years of reporting and going to see my PO, they're called me and released me. I think about how I effed up and wow, it doesn't take much to bring you right back. That why it so important to me that I take my life a day at a time and not take anything for granted. Really what else do I have? That's today, although I retired in 2005. Wow, its been fifthteen years since I retired from my construction union that I'm still active with. I still stay pretty busy with participation, and that's pretty good. It's like having a part time job. It's only four hours a day, and at the end of the month, you get a nice check. I used to think it was only union that does it. Now the carpenters are doing it. It's becoming more prevalent now; we stand with our thirty foot rat In front of a building that's not paying prevailing wage, cutting corners, no bennies as we gather and become a pain for the company we have differences with. We stay there til they become right and put a shop steward on the job because New York City is a union town sign. It's all by law, and then I do a little promotions for my books. I did mention I'm a published author. I can't believe it. I'm blessed. Me? A published author retired from a construction union? I like going to Union Square standing by the train exits as people go in and out. I say to them check it out, check it out, and I give them a card with both books on it—*Rocket & The Construction Worker* and *Beneath the Tracks*. Three books by Jimmy Stalikas. I will soon add *Washington Heights in Search of the Veil*, which will soon be released. Sometimes I think of the where I was. I start to think the only way I could understand the blessing I'll receive is only by his grace. By right, I should have been dead long ago. Even with thirty years clean, I was facing time and still getting in trouble. I was telling my PO that soon I would need to change because I'm moving to the city but at else I'm not getting high. No excuse. Today living in the city with this pandemic, and it's seven in the evening now. There's celebration going out to all the first responders— police, firefighters, mail service, store owners, store workers—because the whole country shut down. It's great when people celebrate people. There's a lot of looting going on; five people died. There was this retired cop who was watching his friend's store, and they shot him. He died at seventy-seven years old. He retired from the police department. He would go to work most of your life protecting people and get shot watching your friend's store. That's effed up.

So as I went to court for shooting the guy in the face after laying up in jail for two weeks, I had to move because we were neighbors. I had to go to anger management. As the judge was turning my file, her face was becoming more upset, and she says to me that if she had her way I'll be going to jail. She asked me if I agreed to many turns as she read them to me, and I said I did. So one day to five years probation.

So I left court and had to go see my PO. As I'm waiting in the waiting area, I see all these people. It's like after thirty years, nothing changed; maybe the area, but it was the same sh—t I dealt with for years. It's funny when I went to court to see my PO, and I went through the metal detectors. The red light went off, and they searched me. Searched my briefcase, and they found a razor knife. Sh—t !I could get f—cked for that. The cop had seen I had a badge, and he said you could pick this up on the way out. I said, "Sure no problem." When I went to see my PO, I took out my wallet, and she saw my son's badge. She asked who shield; I said it was my son's. She said okay. We talked a bit. She assigned me to another PO, so I go to see him a few days. I had to pass to Jamaica, Queens, to the probation office. I see my new PO. We talked. He asked if I did drugs or drink. I said that I don't and have been sober for thirty two years. I make meetings and go out speaking. I mentioned to him if he knew anybody that's looking to get sober to let me know. He said we have all that info, and he shows me a meeting book. I thought that was cool and also said that I was retired. He asked me about my income, and I told him. He then says to bring in when I can, and I did all he asked. I started seeing him every week, then every other week, then once a month. When I stay out of my own way and don't do drugs or drink, things will get better. So it goes on. I always knew I was my worst enemy.

To be honest I don't know how I got this far. It's working with the union in participation as I'm doing right now. I'm still trying to make it happen. I know now I don't have the excitement like I use to have, and that's okay. I'm like coming up on my sixty-eighth birthday in April. Working with the union doing what I have to, living in a nice place, having a puppy, and that's like having a kid; it's work big time and being involved with the union working four hours a day. It's nice; gets you out of the house. So still doing what I can. Been thinking a lot about the spirit world. I don't know that there is another place we go to after this world. I like to think of it as the spirit world where you don't feel pain. Money isn't valued and you are in a sense of timeless warmth—a feeling of serenity. What's beautiful about this is that you can feel this way here. There were times I felt that way here; to be in tune with oneself is everything. I feel I'm changing despite myself. My desires that used to run my life. Today I feel it's not all that important. I use to go out dancing and look to see if I'll meet someone. To be honest, I don't want to meet someone in a club anyway, although I meet girls going to the store for milk or whatever. It's all about timing. Today that's not all that is important. I'm feeling really good in my skin. If I meet someone, fine; if I don't, that's okay too. I must say I go upstate and see my son and grandson. I look at my grandson; he's ten, and I think, *Wow, he's into his game shows he watche*. I think of what I was doing at ten. That goes to show you kids need to be watched. Me? My father wasn't around; my mother worked all day and even til night time. My sisters were into their stuff; my brother was with his friends. Me? I did what the f—ck I wanted. We used to walk over the George Washington Bridge to New Jersey and go to Palisades Amusement Park and steal bikes then ride them back home to the Heights. We'd sell the bikes and do the same sh—t over again until we got caught. Then we would find something else to do. We hit a few cars with luggage and we would find some good stuff like jewelry and all kinds of stuff. That's what we did everyday. I hung out with guys like me. I was robbing bikes, cars, apartments; anything I could do, I did. I think about all the harm that I caused and feel really bad and glad that I got through it. I also know I'm going be paid back in more ways than one. What goes around comes around; it's only a matter of time. I just hope it's not that severe. Whatever comes my way, I got to accept it. I did a lot of sh—t, and sometimes I think, I don't deserve the gifts I get for all the sh—t I've done.

I wasn't right and glad I'm still here to try to make it right. It's all about change. Back in 2012, I had a liver transplant that I would never forget. I tell you as I walk in the hospital at twelve thirty in the morning and seeing my team of doctors who were all there—the doctors I had been seeing thoughout all the test I had been having. I was led to the operating room and was given a shot. The doctor said to count backwards from ten to one. As I laid there courting backwards,

I could see the angels flying above my body. I felt great. The next thing I remember I'm in the O.R. and there's a lot of commotion going on. I'm in the recovery room; I mean it was like a warzone: people getting tagged, people handling other people. The whole experience in the hospital was a time to remember. I'm still making meetings because we do know that meeting is like machine to us in recovery. If there's anything I learned is that: I'm here to help, Jimmy.

Walking Bridge in high circle heights to the Bronx

GWs High School.George Washington H.S

1-6 Grade P.S 189 where the kids sees me playing hooky.

IRT off 191st Subway-going threw the Tunnel

The Tunnel going to Elevator to 191st St. Nick Ave.

Palasades Amusement Park

www.ingramcontent.com/pod-product-compliance
Lightning Source LLC
LaVergne TN
LVHW021742060526
838200LV00052B/3413